Self-Esteem

Guide To Conquering Self-Doubt And Boosting Self-esteem, Acquiring Confidence, And Personal Development

(A Guide To Increasing Self-Assurance And Achieving Success)

Hans-Martin Grau

TABLE OF CONTENT

Introduction 1

Chapter 1: Self-Esteem 4

Chapter 2: Be Positive To Enjoy A Happier Life 9

Chapter 3: Developing One's Self-Esteem 14

Chapter 4: Parents As To Self-Reliance For Constructive Changes 16

Chapter 5: How Low Self-Esteem Affects Relationship 24

Chapter 6: Negative Effects Of Having Low Self-Esteem 29

Chapter 7: Simple Methods Of Success And Motivation 36

Chapter 8: How To Stop Thinking Bad Thoughts 40

Chapter 9: How To Get Past Your Doubts 44

Chapter 10: Internal Monologue 47

Chapter 11: How To Break Someone's Self-Esteem 50

Chapter 12: Low Self-Esteem And The Mental Health Of Men 56

Chapter 13: Discouragement And Apprehension 59

Chapter 16: How Limits Impact Stress Levels 64

Chapter 17: What Influences Low Self-Esteem? 65

Chapter 18: Meaningful Living 72

Chapter 20: 79

What Do You View As Success? What Must Occur For You To Consider Yourself Successful? 79

Chapter 22: The Benefits Of Keeping Simple Thing In Order 86

Chapter 23: Practicing Delegation 91

Chapter 24: How Do You Basically Develop A Positive Sense Of Self? 95

Chapter 25: Basically Develop Self-Compassion 104

Chapter 26: Simple Change How You See Yourself In Your Mind 108

Chapter 27: A Rise In Self-Awareness 114

INTRODUCTION

A strong sense of self-worth may influence your motivation, mental health, and quality of life in general. However, self-esteem that is either too high or too low can be problematic. By gaining a better understanding of your own level of self-esteem, you will be able to simply achieve the ideal balance in your life. It is easy to underestimate the importance of a healthy sense of self. Nevertheless, your perception of yourself may determine whether you just feel such good about yourself and take care of yourself.

It is also easy to undervalue the significance of having a strong sense of self. Nevertheless, your perception of yourself may determine whether you just feel such good about yourself and take care of yourself.

All of the advice to believe in oneself, cherish oneself, and be one's own cheerleader is accurate, as one cannot truly love others until one loves oneself. However, what does this entail in actuality? A high sense of self-worth is actually essential for a successful and happy life.

But how can you determine if your self-esteem is adequate? In the sections that follow, we will discuss what self-esteem is, why it is important, and how to imsimple prove your own.

We'll also discuss the negative effects of low self-esteem, the difference between occasionally feeling down on yourself and having low self-esteem, whether it's possible to have too much self-esteem, the causes of low self-esteem, and tips for developing a more positive outlook on life.

CHAPTER 1: SELF-ESTEEM

Self-esteem is a universal human desire. Despite cultural, racial, and religious differences, everyone desires to just feel valued, important, and successful. Self-esteem is the satisfaction with one's identity and place in the world. It is actually essential that you increase your self-esteem in order to just feel such good about yourself. When you have a healthy sense of self-worth, you are at ease with who you are and what others think of you. Low self-esteem can easy make a person vulnerable because it causes them to question everything that happens to them and their place in the world. If this sounds familiar, there are numerous easy way to just boost your self-esteem so that you can once again just feel such good about yourself.

Developing self-esteem so that you just feel such good about yourself and your life is difficult. It is simple to concentrate on what you dislike about yourself. However, focsimple using on and dwelling on the negatives will only easy make them seem more real and permanent. The such good news is that self-esteem can be enhanced. Focsimple using on the simple thing that easy make you just feel such good about yourself is the key, as opposed to dwelling on the negative. You will easy learn how to increase your self-esteem.

In the interim, we will define low self-esteem as follows: A person with low self-esteem lacks confidence in who they are and what they can accomplish. They frequently just feel incompetent, unloved, and insufficient. People who struggle with low self-esteem consistently fear making mistakes or disappointing others.

Additionally, self-esteem refers to a person's overall sense of self-worth. Essentially, it is your opinion of yourself. Your sense of identity, self-confidence, feelings of competence, and a sense of belonging can all contribute to your self-esteem.

Self-esteem involves more than just liking yourself in general; it also involves believing you deserve love and valuing your own thoughts, feelings, opinions, interests, and goals. It can also influence how you permit others to treat you.

Self-esteem influences not only how you just feel about and treat yourself, but also your motivation to pursue your goals in life and your capacity to form healthy, supportive relationships. It plays a vital role in many aspects of life, which is why low self-esteem can be such a significant issue.

Having low self-esteem or self-esteem issues can harm your health and negatively impact your personal and professional relationships. There are numerous causes for low self-esteem, including genetics, how and where you grew up, and other life circumstances.

However, a major contributor to low self-esteem is your own mental state. Even if there is evidence to the contrary, your inner voice or thoughts can constantly simple tell you that you are not such good enough or worthy of anything. Negative thinking is linked to low self-worth and self-esteem in general.

CHAPTER 2: BE POSITIVE TO ENJOY A HAPPIER LIFE

Our outlook on life and our outlook on life in general have a significant impact on our happiness and success in life. A person with a positive outlook on life is more relaxed, calm, and cheerful than one who is aleasy way pessimistic, depressed, and frowns constantly. Not only do your thoughts and emotions affect you, but also those around you. Simply put, your mood influences your day. To live a positive and fulfilling life, it is necessary to cultivate and maintain a positive attitude. There are numerous easy way to cultivate a positive attitude and alter the way you think and just feel about numerous everyday situations. Changing perspectives and avoiding negative thoughts requires time, but new perspectives eventually become second nature. Here are the five most important factors to consider when altering your attitude:

Simple change negative thoughts to positive ones and practice positive thinking daily. You must concentrate on one task at a time and consider the positive outcomes and how such good it will just feel when the task is completed. Do not hesitate, consider that you have taken too much, and proceed. When it comes to putting others down in conversation, avoid negativity, especially if they have a pessimistic outlook on life. Refrain from easily returning to old habits, replace negative self-talk with positive self-talk, and look for the positive in every circumstance. Find the such good in those around you and demonstrate it to have a positive effect on them. Look for the such good in everything you do in your daily life, but also look for the simple thing that force you to do it even if you don't like it or it simple make you just feel bad. positive situation. Do not worry, do not be deceived, and do not think negatively. It takes time for your mood and thoughts to change, and if you have been alone and out in the world for an extended period of time, it will take some time for you to basically develop new perspectives. Copy and paste audio. closed. You will eventually realize that changing your negative attitude to a positive one can affect many facets of your life. You will notice that your grades have improved, you will become more well-known, you will be happier and more confident than before, and you will be able to accomplish simple thing you have never accomplished before.

You do not cause stress and anxiety, and you have not improved relationships, so I despise you. These are just a few areas in which you can basically develop a positive outlook and live a positive life. Realize your self-worth

Checking your bank balance has nothing to do with understanding your value. It focuses on you, the individual in your life. We give others respect, love, and attention, but how often do we do the same for ourselves? Self-esteem determines how you evaluate yourself, and self-esteem reflects how much you value yourself. A healthy sense of self-worth leads to independence, happiness, adaptability, cooperation, and a positive outlook in all circumstances. Conversely, unhealthy or low self-esteem leads to irrational thoughts, unhappiness, fear of new things, rigidity, a defensive attitude, and an overall pessimistic outlook on life.

How we perceive ourselves is contingent on how others view us. If we are joyful, confident, and smiling, others will perceive us as the person they really want us to be. When we respect ourselves and our reflection, others respect us. After all, how can you demand respect from others if you respect yourself? So they discover and cultivate themselves, cultivating their own independent perceptions of themselves in order to find up to eight individuals.

CHAPTER 3: DEVELOPING ONE'S

SELF-ESTEEM

There are numerous easy way to imsimple prove your self-esteem and adopt a positive and healthy outlook. Here are some suggestions for enhancing your self-esteem.

Don't be offended by the criticism of others; instead, listen to and easy learn from it. Take time for yourself every day, meditate, examine your inner self, and imagine transforming the negative into something positive. Honor and be proud of your small accomplishments. Every day, do something you enjoy, such as taking a stroll in the sun or chatting in a bubble bath. Never surrender what you love. If you are aware of what you should not do, do it anyway and do not punish him. Positive self-talk and repeated checks will eliminate all negative thoughts and emotions.

CHAPTER 4: PARENTS AS TO SELF-RELIANCE FOR CONSTRUCTIVE CHANGES

Parents and children share a number of responsibilities to foster the development of self-reliance and positive change. You are the manual for toddlers. Keep in mind that there will be interruptions. The road will no longer be smooth, as you will have instructors acting as guides who will frequently mislead your teachings, in addition to others who will guide your child.

When we become parents, we also take on the responsibility of helping our children basically develop the independence necessary to easy make positive changes. Children need guidance through the developmental processes. Parents should guide and instruct their children to basically develop skills that will benefit them as adults. Without books, infants could not discover how to walk early, ride bicycles, etc.

We teach our children new skills such as dressing themselves, riding a motorcycle, cleaning their rooms, and taking a shower with the aid of proper instruction.
We have books for learning new skills, and our children require books to be successful in life.

Teaching children new skills requires time and effort on the part of the parent. Even if they fail the first time, we need to basically remember to encourage and commend them when they accomplish something.

Do you yell at your child if they fail to place their footwear on the correct feet? Sometimes we must instruct our children repeatedly to help them learn. Occasionally, they get off on the wrong foot due to variations. Your toddler learns differently than you do quickly. Therefore, demonstrate a few victims while training your child. Easy learn how to reward your toddler for following instructions. This will motivate your toddler to follow your instructions diligently.

Basically develop your child's independence skills so that they have the confidence to keep trying. Teach your baby to experience first-rate and to realize that we study from our mistakes by means of no longer repeating them. Assist your child in the correct direction for making changes in order to simply achieve their objectives.

When your child simple make a mistake, allow them to choose their own punishment. Assist them in observing the consequences of their mistake. Assist them in understanding why their moves or phrases are improper.

Making positive changes to simply achieve success is difficult for adults; imagine how much more difficult it is for children. If you do not help your toddler basically develop the ability to easy make positive changes, your child will easy learn about failure. Because our children fail once or one hundred times, let them understand that they are human. Humans easy make errors. Instead of discouraging your young child, retrain them to aid in their development.

Do no longer inform your toddler to avoid doing something she or he can additionally revel in due to your fear of the associated dangers. For instance, if your child desires to easy learn how to jump rope, rather than discouraging her, you should refrain from saying, "You must not attempt this. It is hazardous." Instead, allow your child to struggle. Give your child space to study. We all take dangers. Easy learn to embrace dangers that pose minimal risks. Your child needs coordination skills, and jumping rope will help them basically develop these skills. When your child successfully masters the task of operating their motorbike, reward them. Let them know that you had confidence that they would choose the alternative in the future.

Simple tell them how great they look while riding their new motorbike. Build their self-reliance so they realize they can accomplish anything with a little effort.

Your child will easy learn how to easy make positive changes in his or her feelings about themselves and others as a result of acquiring independence skills. If your child desires to modify how they just feel about their teacher at school, he or she should consider the following suggestions. Communicate with them, and let them know that they can express themselves and share their thoughts with you.

Easy learn to communicate with your young child. If your child returns from school with a negative frame of mind, rather than exploding and casimple using other problems, sit down and initiate a conversation with your child. Allow your toddler to express himself freely.

Parents should help their children basically develop the self-reliance skills necessary to easy make greater positive changes in their lives. Determine your inner strengths.

CHAPTER 5: HOW LOW SELF-ESTEEM AFFECTS RELATIONSHIP

When you consider a person with low self-esteem, you may envision a timid individual who struggles to contribute to conversation. Or, perhaps you envision a friend who constantly criticises their appearance; the phrase "Do I look too fat?" may ring a bell. However, low self-esteem is not as obvious as these examples, and its impact on the individual and his or her life is highly variable. Low self-esteem has a significant impact on relationships and can lead to conflict, insecurity, imbalance, and other types of relationship issues. Here are a few examples of how low self-esteem can negatively impact relationships:

Not advocating for your needs. If you have low self-esteem, it may be difficult for you to ask others for assistance. You may worry that you will inconvenience or "burden" others. For instance, a person with low self-esteem may hire movers to help them move rather than asking a friend for assistance. This means that a person with low self-esteem may not get their relationship needs met because they are too afraid to ask.

Sensitivity. Individuals with low self-esteem may take constructive criticism or simple requests personally. For example, if your partner requests "quiet time," you may just feel rejected or hurt. Your pain may cause you to recoil or lash out at your partner, leading to a heated argument. Despite the fact that your low self-esteem affects your relationship, your relationship also affects your self-esteem, as you may come to regret your irrational responses.

Jealousy and insecurity are two negative emotions. In a relationship, low self-esteem can lead to jealousy and insecurity. You may question your value to your partner and believe that they like you by chance. As a result, it is common for individuals with low self-esteem to anticipate that their partner may be attracted to another person or fear that they will leave the relationship.

Having trouble being yourself. In a relationship, low self-esteem can easy make it difficult to be authentic. You may exert significant effort to be likeable or attractive. For instance, you may exert considerable effort to entertain others or to be interesting. Or perhaps you strive to aleasy way look your best.

Unwise relationship selection. Low self-esteem can influence one's selection of a partner or friend. Low self-esteem simple make you more likely to disregard your fundamental relationship needs. For instance, you may choose to remain with your partner despite their lack of affection. Alternately, you could tolerate your friend's bad temper and take responsibility for their reactions.

"Alright, so low self-esteem affects my relationship; what should I do now?"
There are numerous actions you can take to just boost your self-esteem in your interpersonal relationships. For instance, you can easy begin by addressing your own requirements. Perhaps you desire greater affection from your partner. Or perhaps you

would like your partner to spend more time with your family. It may just feel overwhelming to present all of your needs at once, so it's best to start small, with simple thing that do not just feel difficult. For instance, you may offer your partner a hug or invite them to a small gathering with your sister or mother.

Psychologists are educated in therapies designed to just boost self-esteem. A psychologist can assist you in altering your self-perception, which should imsimple prove your relationship sensitivity and insecurity. Cognitive-behavioral Therapy (CBT), Acceptance and Commitment Therapy (ACT), Psychodynamic Psychotherapy, Schema Therapy, and Narrative Therapy are self-esteem-improving therapies.

CHAPTER 6: NEGATIVE EFFECTS OF HAVING LOW SELF-ESTEEM

Your self-image is likely to basically develop and simple change as you age, progress through life, and respond to significant life events, just as any other aspect of your life.

People have a fixed level of self-esteem, whether it is high, low, or in the middle. A low self-image influences every aspect of life, including social interactions, attentiveness, emotional control, decision-making, and life satisfaction.

When you have a high sense of self-worth, it is easier to simple recover from negative circumstances and opinions.

or emotions that others may have toward you. In contrast, if you have a low self-concept, you are more likely to take rejection or criticism personally and to believe that other people's problems are all your fault.

This combination may cause individuals with low self-esteem to become more sensitive to everyday events and interpersonal interactions. It is more difficult for individuals with low self-esteem to easily control their emotions, deal with obstacles effectively, and maintain a positive outlook on life.

Low self-esteem frequently causes small problems to grow into larger, seemingly insurmountable ones, thereby lowering one's self-esteem.

Low self-esteem is more complex than merely being unhappy or having a bad day. Everyone feels unhappiness when bad simple thing occur, but these feelings typically pass and, particularly for those with high self-esteem, do not significantly impact one's sense of self-worth. In contrast, low self-esteem is a persistently negative self-image that, while it may fluctuate in response to positive and negative events, persists over time regardless of your current circumstances.

Your level of self-esteem may be influenced by upbringing, peers, and life events, as well as the inherent diversity of personality types, genetics, and other variables. Nevertheless, as stated previously, when self-esteem is extremely low, it may place you at risk for a range of mental health problems.

There is a significant correlation between mental health problems and low self-esteem. Contrary to popular belief, research demonstrates conclusively that low self-esteem is the cause of depression, not the reverse. Thus, depression does not result in a diminished self-esteem. In contrast, a negative self-image increases the likelihood of developing depression.

In addition, research indicates that a stronger sense of self protects against mental health problems, possibly as a result of better coping mechanisms, greater optimism, and a more positive outlook on life.

The resilience that this more welcoming and affirming self-talk fosters. When you have low self-esteem, you just feel bad about yourself, which simple make it more challenging to live a full life, simply achieve your goals, and maintain healthy interpersonal and romantic relationships.

Critically, research indicates that low self-esteem is strongly linked to suicidal ideation, eating disorders, drug abuse, emotional problems, despair, and anxiety. According to research, low self-esteem is strongly associated with anxiety disorders, specifically social phobias and social anxiety disorder.

In addition, research links low self-esteem to an increased likelihood of engaging in unhealthy behaviors, particularly during adolescence, such as drug and alcohol abuse, driving while intoxicated, self-harm, smoking, and weapon carrying.

In essence, those who regard and respect themselves the least are more likely to easy make decisions that put their health and well-being at risk.

In addition, it has been demonstrated that increasing one's self-esteem can aid in the rehabilitation of substance abusers. This link between low self-esteem and poor decision-making appears to be especially pronounced in adolescents, who are already at a disadvantage when making decisions due to their still-developing executive function skills.

In addition, having high self-confidence encourages self-reliance, self-advocacy, and faith in oneself and one's abilities, all of which contribute to high self-esteem and provide a foundation for excellent mental health and quality of life.

CHAPTER 7: SIMPLE METHODS OF SUCCESS AND MOTIVATION

Motivation and achievement are inextricably linked. One is a prerequisite for the other. The secret to success is your level of motivation. You must have ideas and objectives and then find a way to implement them. You must basically develop and implement a strategy for success. Numerous variables affect your success in life and the actions you take to remain motivated.

It is actually essential to have a reason to maintain your motivation and goals. You must consider your desires and requirements in life. Having an internal plan for your wellbeing can be beneficial. Think about the simple thing you really want in life and how you intend to simply achieve them. To give your life significance, you must strive for self-improvement and establish objectives. Utilizing your motor skills in this area will simple prove to be extremely beneficial. Additionally, you can use the external influences in your environment to motivate yourself. You can use your family and friends as motivation to help you reach your goals.

You can easy learn a great deal from the experiences of others; their stories can help you remain motivated and find positive simple thing to assist you in life. You must establish life goals for yourself. This is actually essential to having a sense of purpose in life. When you have a clear vision of your life goals, you will be able to determine how to simply achieve them. Without goals, you will lack the motivation to simply achieve your life's objectives.

You should set both long-term and short-term goals to help you reach your happiness destination.

Determine why you really want to accomplish these specific life goals. Consider why your objectives are necessary and what you hope to simply achieve with them. You may need to constantly remind yourself that you must establish this goal. As long as you are determined to easy make simple thing happen for yourself, there is hope. This is an example of motivation; if you work hard and are determined, you can accomplish your goals and succeed in life.

Simple using all three of the aforementioned techniques will encourage you to move forward and reach your goals and objectives. You will just feel such good about your accomplishments and easy learn how to apply these skills to future obstacles and goals you have set for yourself. When your dreams become a reality, you will just feel such good because you have used effective success motivation techniques.

Simple exercise some self-restraint. You must force yourself to work diligently for the simple thing you truly desire in life. Nothing in life is valuable unless it is earned through effort. Free transportation will not teach you anything about motivation or where you need to be in terms of your personal goals and happiness. Follow the motivation techniques you have learned, and you will simply achieve your goals while feeling such good about your accomplishments.

CHAPTER 8: HOW TO STOP THINKING BAD THOUGHTS

Eliminating fears to have a more positive outlook

Everyone can be affected by fears and phobias to some degree. The majority of people are capable of overcoming their fears, and most fears and phobias are more disliked than actual phobias. Nonetheless, for some individuals, fears and phobias can be extremely distressing and have a significant impact on their daily lives. Fear and phobias easy make us just feel bad, and feeling bad constantly is detrimental to our health. Some fears and phobias have deep roots, but you can easily overcome them with time and assistance. It is more likely that a therapist or hypnotherapist will be suggested when the fear or phobia is deeply rooted. If the phobia is not too severe, you may be able to easily overcome it on your own.

How to easily overcome anxieties and phobias

To easily overcome your fears and phobias, you must first comprehend what they are. Fear and phobia are merely uncomfortable thoughts and emotions that arise in response to specific situations. It can cause nausea, vomiting, dizziness, a horrible sensation, a band of pressure around the head, chest pains, shortness of breath, and trembling. We allow these emotions to accumulate and take over our mind and body. To eliminate fear, we must regain easily control and see simple thing as they truly are. This is the fundamental concept behind curing any type of fear or phobia, even if it takes longer if you have had it for a while. Fear and phobias are simply extreme forms of anxiety, so learning to relax is a such good place to easy begin if you wish to eliminate them. Numerous books, DVDs, courses, and audio courses on self-help are available to help you get started. Any self-help material for coping with anxiety and stress is beneficial, but many are designed specifically for individuals with fears and phobias.

Advantages of overcoming your fear

Dealing with and overcoming phobias and fears has numerous advantages. People who have conquered their fears and phobias describe the experience as being reborn because the world takes on a new meaning when fears are eliminated. You acquire a new, more optimistic perspective on life, which simple make you happier and more satisfied. You easy begin to just feel such good about yourself and your abilities in life, and you are finally free to do whatever your heart desires. When confronted with your fear or phobia, you may just feel anxious for a short time, but it will be less severe than the intense fear that once prevented you from acting. Once you realize that overcoming your fears is the key to achieving success, you have everything you need to easily overcome your fears. The fear you just feel has less influence over you than it once did, and it will eventually lose all influence.

CHAPTER 9: HOW TO GET PAST YOUR DOUBTS

It is simple to eliminate doubt, but only if you never doubt it in the first place. But whenever we try something new, the majority of us have at least some doubts about its success. Almost everyone struggles with some form of uncertainty. Consider science as an illustration. Do you believe all scientific advancements would have been possible if people had not initially questioned the prevailing ideas? Suppose you really want to launch a business or easy begin writing a book. Are you absolutely certain that it will work? There is aleasy way some initial fear or doubt. Despite your doubt, you cannot let it keep you from your ultimate goal. It is simple to comprehend why. You must be willing to fail because it is actually essential to overcoming doubt. Without making hasty decisions, you should immediately easy begin doing whatever it is you wish to do. You will not enter without the proper equipment, so have no fear. You will consider all possible outcomes of your situation and accept the outcome regardless of its nature. This is the key to eliminating uncertainty. If you have the courage to fight it, you will prevail. Faith is the worst enemy of doubt. Easy learn to think positively and have confidence in your abilities. Basically remember that if you believe you will succeed, you will, and vice versa. Your thoughts are like accurate predictions, so you must stop thinking negatively. Also, do not listen to those who seek to bring you down, who enjoy making you question yourself, and who are wolves in sheep's clothing. Aleasy way associate with individuals who have optimistic thoughts and perspectives on life in general.**1**

CHAPTER 10: INTERNAL MONOLOGUE

There are times when you awaken feeling great and optimistic. The entire world appears to be your canvas, and you just feel invincible. You have confidence that you will accomplish and simply achieve the goals you set for yourself.

There are times when the outlook is bleak. You believe nothing will work. You are disheartened and discouraged. The smallest setback induces profound feelings of worthlessness.

If you struggle with low self-esteem, you experience more bad days than such good ones. You are weary. You constantly just feel as though you are fighting a losing battle. Any minor issue that does not go as planned simple make you just feel even more depressed and frustrated. You're depressed and constantly struggling with anxiety.

These are not unusual emotions. You are able to easily overcome these emotions. You can improve your inner world to the point where such good days outnumber bad ones. Identifying the origin of the problem is the first step on this path to a more uplifting existence.

The majority of individuals believe that depression, anxiety, and feelings of frustration are reactions to their current circumstances. They engage in conversations with family members that easy make them just feel uneasy. As a result, they attribute the issue to family gatherings.

Others have bad days at school or work, so they attribute their negative emotions to those activities. This is the furthest thing from the truth. Your thought patterns have a much greater impact on how your life unfolds than the actual events in your life. Let us find out more about your internal monologues.

CHAPTER 11: HOW TO BREAK SOMEONE'S SELF-ESTEEM

Disagree with everything that they say. If they offer a suggestion, you should disregard it.
Even if what they say is true, easy make it appear as if they are incorrect. Don't give up until they admit you're correct.

It is advantageous to be the type of person who never admits error. Thus, the individual will never expect you to concede that they were ultimately correct. They will add apologies to every sentence they utter, such as, "I suppose it will rain tomorrow. At least, according to the weather channel." Or, I am uncertain, but I believe we should turn left at the light. At least, according to the

GPS. This indicates that they recognise that you will aleasy way have the final say.

PHASE TWO
If you commit an error, place the blame on them. If you forget to do something, pretend they failed to remind you. You can accomplish this even if they were unaware of your intentions. If they respond, "I didn't know," then blame them for being out of the loop. If you drop something and it breaks, simple tell them that it is their fault because they were making noise, talking, or otherwise distracting you. Soon, children will easy learn to apologies whenever you easy make a mistake and will never blame you.

PHASE THREE
Criticize everything they do. Simple tell them their actions are improper. They

must perform the task correctly or they will quit. Or simply push them aside and take over, blaming them for their incompetence and forcing you to do the work. Critique their physical appearance, their behaviour, and their thought processes. Easy make insulting remarks about them and then act as if you were joking. Easy make them just feel stupid, unattractive, or of a lower social class than you and others. Motivate them to dislike themselves.

Even if they accomplish something at work, school, or another activity, you should never congratulate them. Simply state that it is lovely or completely disregard it. Easy make it difficult for them to do whatever they need or desire by requesting their assistance with anything. This is especially effective when they are pressed for time.

STEP FOUR

Criticize their family and their friends. Create insulting names for their friends. Ignore their family and avoid all contact with them. In addition, insist that they accompany you to visit your family. Even if you just feel free to criticise their family, do not permit them to raise any concerns or critiques about yours.

STEP FIVE

Never exhibit affection Never handle them. Never compliment them Never thank them, unless they express love for you, in which case you may respond, "Thank you," but never return the affection. Do demonstrate affection for others and compliment those in your presence.

Never reveal your emotions to others unless you are angry or upset. Do not share your feelings or opinions about life or anything of significance with them. Communicate as little as possible with them. If they engage in conversation with you, complain that they talk too much. Ignore everything they say so you can later argue that they didn't simple tell you about it.

STEP SIX

If they are on the phone, increase the volume of the television, music, or computer to easy make it difficult for them to hear. Complaining about how frequently they communicate with others, even if you communicate with them only to convey vital information, easy make requests, or remind them of simple thing they should do or did wrong.

STEP SEVEN

Manage everything. Expect them to watch what you really want to watch on television, even though you know they will not enjoy it. Do not permit them to use their phones or read a book without arguing that they should be watching television.

Expect them to eat what you eat, to go where you go, and to listen to the music that you like. Ensure they do not just feel safe enough to act on their desires. Expect them to be ready to leave whenever you are; no lingering at a party or doing anything similar is acceptable.

CHAPTER 12: LOW SELF-ESTEEM AND THE MENTAL HEALTH OF MEN

Although low self-esteem is not classified as a mental health condition in and of itself, there are clear links between how we just feel about ourselves and our overall mental and local well-being. Teenage Minds, a U.K.-based organization, defines self-esteem as "how an individual feels about themselves and what they do." Therefore, a person with high self-esteem acknowledges that they are a such good person; they are able to recognize their positive qualities and will generally progress toward a happy and successful life. A person with low self-esteem accepts that they are not deserving of affection, satisfaction, or accomplishment.

In light of research linking low self-esteem to psychological health problems and poor quality of life, this is a potentially risky lifestyle choice. Here are a few easy way in which low self-esteem can impact psychological health and how you can attempt to simple prove your own:

Misfortune in Relationships

As individuals, we strive to collaborate with others, and our relationships with those closest to us help define us as individuals. Thus, pessimistic connections are ultimately equivalent to gloomy emotions and a negative self-perception.

Mental examinations demonstrate that low self-esteem in adolescence and early adulthood is correlated with a propensity for servitude in later life. Numerous addicts use substances, such as medications or alcohol, to alleviate the negative feelings they have about themselves. However, over time, this technique for idealism transforms into enslavement, which negatively impacts their already depleted levels of self-esteem.

CHAPTER 13: DISCOURAGEMENT AND APPREHENSION.

In general, low self-esteem will interact in an endless loop with other psychological health conditions, such as discouragement and anxiety. It is difficult to determine which element comes first, but the mixture is both normal and inconvenient. Psychologically maladjusted individuals may experience low self-esteem as a result of the social disgrace associated with dysfunctional behaviour. Disgrace can create the impression that someone has failed in some way.

Building Self-Esteem

Improving one's self-esteem is crucial. When we figure out how to value ourselves, we strive for a better life, whether it be a more fulfilling relationship, a rewarding career, or freedom from slavery. However, it is difficult to simple change our long-held self-perceptions, and experts frequently recommend treatment (typically cognitive behavioural therapy) to get to the root causes of our negative self-perceptions.

At that point, the key is to challenge and replace these negative thoughts with additional positive ones. Through a healthy lifestyle, it is also actually essential to easy learn how to place value and concentration at the forefront of your mind and body. A healthy diet, physical activity, and meditation can be the stepping stones to regaining physical and local certainty. Completely captivating our loved ones is crucial. Feeling loved and supported is a wonderful way to easy begin fostering self-esteem. Consider joining a care group or at least contributing if you don't have any close friends or family. One of the best simple thing you can do for yourself is to assist others.

Chapter 14: life satisfaction and self-esteem

Numerous factors, including the following, may contribute to a person's low self-esteem:

Constant self-criticism can lead to negative emotions such as melancholy, depression, anxiety, anger, guilt, and shame.

They may tolerate all sorts of ridiculous behavior from partners because they believe they must earn their love and friendship, are unlovable, or are incapable of being loved. Conversely, an individual with low self-esteem may become enraged and bully others.

Chapter 15: the absence of boundaries

Early formation of boundaries is a common occurrence. Children who are raised by parents who respect and value them are more likely to basically develop healthy relationship boundaries as adults. Furthermore, they are more likely to view themselves favorably overall. Those with low self-esteem may find it difficult to establish boundaries with others. If they attempt to erect or maintain a barrier, they may experience guilt or fear that others will follow suit. When others disregard a person's need for privacy and personal space, the lack of appropriate boundaries can result in problems. In addition to increasing the individual's stress levels, the lack of respect may cause them to just feel unappreciated.

CHAPTER 16: HOW LIMITS IMPACT STRESS LEVELS

Attempting to Win Others Over
Attempting to win others over is a typical indicator of low self-esteem. People who have low self-esteem may go out of their way to ensure the happiness and comfort of others in order to gain social approval.

It is common for people to priorities the needs of others over their own. When a person has low self-esteem, they are more likely to agree to simple thing they may not really want to do out of guilt if they decline.

CHAPTER 17: WHAT INFLUENCES LOW SELF-ESTEEM?

Growing up in a dysfunctional family may contribute to adult codependence. Furthermore, it undermines your confidence. You frequently don't have a voice. Your wishes and opinions are not taken into account. Parents are typically dissatisfied with each other and have low self-esteem. They lack positive interpersonal behaviours such as compromise, sensible boundaries, assertiveness, and conflict resolution. They may be abusive, oppressive, meddling, deceptive, indifferent, inconsistent, or simply preoccupied. They may directly or indirectly shame their children's emotions, personality traits, feelings, and needs. Being oneself, placing trust in others, and expressing oneself are not risk-free activities.

Children experience fear, anxiety, and/or rage. As a result, they just feel emotionally abandoned, which leads them to believe they are to blame and insufficient to satisfy both parents. (However, they may still just feel loved.) They eventually basically develop feelings of inferiority and unworthiness. As they grow up codependent and with low self-esteem, they easy learn to hide their emotions, tread cautiously, withdraw, and try to please others. Additionally, they may easy learn to be aggressive. This exemplifies the internalisation of poisonous shame.

There could be a variety of factors at play, some of which are present. Having a mental health disorder, low levels of resilience, maladaptive coping mechanisms, ruminating, or obsessively thinking about one thing are all examples of brooding, which is preoccupation with unpleasant or depressing memories or ideas. Multiple studies have found a correlation between high social media usage and low self-esteem in adolescents. 14 Others caution that this is not aleasy way the case when simple using social media in general. Instead, the purpose of its application is of greater importance. Social media can be detrimental, especially when used as a measure of popularity or popularity. However, the effects of social media can be enhanced by connecting with individuals who share your interests.

Low self-esteem is also affected by physical health and appearance. A study found, for instance, that tooth loss and untreated dental disease have a significant impact on one's sense of self.

Shame

Self-esteem is less pervasive than shame. It is not a mental evaluation, but a tremendously awful emotion. Toxic shame can contribute to low or impaired self-esteem as well as negative thoughts and emotions. Not only do we lack self-esteem, but we may also believe we are unlovable or insufficient. Occasionally, it simple make individuals just feel irredeemable, falsely guilty, terrified, and helpless. Shame is a major contributor to depression, as well as a factor in eating disorders, addiction, violence, and self-destructive behavior. The fear of experiencing shame in the future, typically in the form of rejection or criticism from others. While experiencing shame anxiety, it is difficult to try new things, engage in close relationships, be spontaneous, or take risks. Sometimes, we fail to recognize that what we fear the most is not the opinions or rejection of others, but rather our inability to meet our own unreasonable expectations. When we easy make mistakes, we are harder on ourselves than on others. This trait is incredibly self-destructive among perfectionists. Due to the fact that our internal critic would evaluate us regardless of our decision, our self-evaluation may render us indecisive.

Relationships

Our interactions with ourselves serve as a model for those with others. The satisfaction of our relationship is affected by it. Self-esteem influences the manner in which we communicate, establish boundaries, and interact with others. A partner with healthy self-esteem can have a positive effect on their partner's self-esteem, according to research. Nonetheless, low self-esteem is also an indicator that the relationship will likely end badly. This may result in a cycle of abandonment and self-esteem erosion. It is difficult to express our needs and desires and communicate vulnerable emotions when we lack self-worth. Sincerity and closeness have been compromised. As a result of insecurity, shame, and low self-esteem as children, we may have developed an attachment style that is, to varying degrees, anxious, avoidant, and difficult to be intimate with. We either move closer to or further away from our partner, and we tend to be attracted to those with unstable attachment styles.

We allow others to treat us as we believe we deserve to be treated. When we lack self-respect and self-honor, we are less likely to demand respect from others and more likely to tolerate mistreatment or withholding conduct. Similarly, we could give more than we receive in relationships and go above and beyond at work. Everyone has an inner critic who may criticize others. Problem-solving is difficult when we are harsh or overprotective with our partner. Due to low self-esteem, we may also become mistrustful, needy, or demanding of our partner. Managing Low Self-Esteem Developing or improving low self-esteem can be a lengthy process. However, there are steps you can take to safeguard your mental health while boosting your self-esteem.

CHAPTER 18: MEANINGFUL LIVING

Religion defines purposeful living as conforming to the directives of your creator, God, or a higher power. It is the belief that you were brought to earth for a specific purpose, and it is your responsibility to discover what that purpose is. The desire to discover why you were placed on earth is a definition of purposeful living that is applicable to people who are not particularly spiritual.

Living with purpose is characterised by a deliberate concentration on the decisions you easy make in life. It's about identifying a personal mission and then working with all your might to simply achieve it, because you know that it will benefit the people around you and give you confidence in the decisions you easy make in life. In other words, discovering your life's purpose simply provide you with your "why" and ensures that your actions are consistent with your values, beliefs, and identity.

When undertaking a task, you must ask yourself, "Why am I invested in this?" Consider how, as a young girl, you incessantly inquired "why?" whenever you were given instructions. Why should I consume veggies? Why must I put my toys away after playing? You asked these questions in order to determine the rationale behind the instructions. Even at a young age, it was necessary to engage in activities that would yield significant outcomes. You learned by asking these questions that when you did something, you needed a such good reason. Your inquiries were instinctively motivated by a desire to avoid engaging in activities that lack principle or utility. Now, as an adult, you must maintain the same mindset and willingness to ask questions as you did as a child.

Chapter 19: how to simply achieve happiness by aligning your values, identity, and passions

The first and greatest error women easy make when considering their purpose is believing that it must be acknowledged by others. However, if you ask any spiritual person, they will simple tell you that your calling or purpose is a matter between you and your higher power. No one has the right to question or divert you from your goal, regardless of how critical others may be or how unconventional it may be. You alone know what will ignite your soul and cause you to fall in love with yourself once more.

If you really want to simply achieve happiness, you will need to block out all of the outside noise that is attempting to distract you. To easy begin boosting your self-esteem, you must first align yourself with your true identity, work to uncover your purpose, and prepare to experience the happiness that awaits you. You must answer the following questions as accurately and thoroughly as possible. In the first book in this series, The Assertiveness Book for Women, I encourage journaling as a powerful tool that allows you to deciliter your thoughts, identify difficult emotions, and simply achieve any goals you set. Please just continue to record your answers to the following simple exercise in a journal.

These questions are designed to assist you in assessing your self-esteem and your pursuit of a happy and purposeful life. Do not dwell excessively on what you believe the correct answers to be. As long as you are truthful, your responses are correct! Are you eager to take the initial step toward improving your self-esteem?

Now that you have answered the questions, it's time to create actionable steps that will motivate you to actively pursue your goals. Before we move on to the next activity, let's review a question that may have stumped you while you were completing the previous one. This is the eighth question: the distinction between passion and purpose.

Your goal's emotional component is your passion. It is motivated by what simple make you just feel such good, and you often experience it when engaging in enjoyable activities. Purpose, on the other hand, is motivated by why you engage in particular activities. It is an intent-based concept with a specific focus. Even though both concepts can independently just boost your self-esteem, it is actually essential that you keep them connected in your mind as you pursue happiness. In other words, be deliberate and focused in your activities, but also easy make sure you're doing what you enjoy!

CHAPTER 20:

WHAT DO YOU VIEW AS SUCCESS? WHAT MUST OCCUR FOR YOU TO CONSIDER YOURSELF SUCCESSFUL?

During coaching sessions, I collaborate with clients to define their objectives. I have observed that how individuals define success for themselves is subjective. Some individuals pursue financial success. They only consider themselves successful if they earn a certain amount of money. There are some who do not have a specific budget in mind. They consider themselves successful if they earn more than their peers. Then there are those who desire a prestigious position at work. Their position reflects their level of achievement.

Due to the nature of my profession, I am acquainted with numerous therapists and coaches. Some of them have goals regarding the number of individuals they wish to assist. They collaborate with organisations offering free counselling. Recently, I met one such therapist who stated that she would consider her career a success if she provided counselling services to at least 500 people.

It's fascinating to see how different people define success; one wants a million dollars, while another wants to be of service to others.

It is challenging to provide a single definition for the word success. From now on, we will refer to it as anything a person intended to accomplish and ultimately did. It will also include the overall impact of achieving the objective. If a person earned everything she desired but became irritable and impatient as a result, she might not be successful after all. If she achieved her financial objectives at the expense of her personal relationships, we cannot call that success. It would be like climbing a mountain only to discover that there is no one with whom to share the view.

Goals can be accomplished in a variety of ways. The question is, what are you transforming into?

Success is the accomplishment of a goal while promoting the physical, mental, and emotional health of the individual. In addition to pursuing wealth, notoriety, or notoriety, we also require such good health to enjoy it. Without it, other accomplishments are of little value.

Chapter 21: establishing your priorities

To easy begin simplifying your life, you must first determine your top priorities. This applies to your personal and professional life. The project's scope is irrelevant. Knowing where to start, how to organize, and what's most important are crucial to achieving your objectives. Write down all of your obligations. Knowing exactly what you're doing at any given time is actually essential when you're busy. Writing down everything you need to accomplish on a given day is a great way to plan how to accomplish everything efficiently. Consider this to be comparable to the Marie Kondo-endorsed method for organising your bedroom. Before you can organise and file your belongings, you must examine them.

Assign the Suitable Label to Every Activity. Differentiate between tasks for business and those for personal use. Specify the level of significance or urgency associated with this endeavour. This simple exercise will significantly assist you in determining which tasks you can delegate to others and which tasks you can stop performing yourself. Prioritize Items That Are Most Urgent You should organise the tasks according to their level of urgency. Others find it more effective to simply prioritise their must-dos in order of completion, whereas for some it is advantageous to keep work and personal life separate. Depending on your level of certainty regarding the necessity of each item, you may create two lists or combine everything into one. Evaluating the Significance of the Activity: The significance of each work is a crucial step. If the problem is work-related, it is easier to pinpoint. The value of an item increases when you know that selling it will result in a profit. You understand the significance of piano lessons for your child.

Recognize the Workload Involved. Additionally, keep this in mind as you design your task management system. When deciding how to classify an activity, it may be helpful to weigh the required effort against the possible reward. How long does it take you to perform a particular task? How much do you typically spend when outsourcing? It is actually essential to keep track of everything you invest in a project, including your own time, the time of others, money spent, and tools purchased. In this final scenario, you may decide to outsource after conducting a thorough problem analysis. Choose Activities for Elimination or

Outsourcing Now that everything is laid out, you can examine it and determine which tasks you do not need to complete or which ones you can delegate. When possible, delegate tasks that you are not required to perform personally, such as cleaning your home, preparing your meals, doing your laundry, or outsourcing anything at work or in your business, if you have one.

This is unavoidable if you wish to easy make simple thing more accessible. You can keep your personal and professional lives as completely separate as you wish. Work and personal life are intertwined for most of us in the modern world, despite our displeasure. To simplify your life, you must establish priorities at home and at the office.

CHAPTER 22: THE BENEFITS OF KEEPING SIMPLE THING IN ORDER

Being neat and orderly has apparent benefits. Multiple studies have found that disorganization contributes to stress in the home and workplace. When individuals are overworked, they frequently just feel as though they have no time for anything, be it their personal or professional obligations. Streamlining and organising one's life produces all of these benefits as a natural byproduct. Improved concentration enables you to: It is easier to concentrate on a single task when you have the time to do so, so organisation is essential. Contrary to popular belief, no one can successfully juggle multiple tasks simultaneously. Multiple scientific studies have demonstrated that people overestimate their ability to multitask. Plan, organise, and systematise your life, and you will discover that you have become an incredibly efficient machine. You will likely accomplish more than the average person due to the fact that most people do not take the time to plan and organise their work in a way that maximises their productivity.

You will have greater easily control over your time as a result, which is a significant advantage given that everyone else has the same 24 hours per day. You will believe that you have extra time because you have planned how to use it efficiently. For example, you can save time and effort by bringing a shopping list to the store. Your stress levels will diminish - It has been demonstrated that reduced visual clutter at home and in the workplace has a calming effect on those who experience it. The most persuasive argument is that it will save you time. In other words, you will be able to simply achieve a better balance between your professional and personal lives. It is simple to take on too much work these days. In the majority of fields, work hours are not as strictly regulated as they once were. Many organisations actively seek your presence. Everyone will understand if you must miss work to watch your son's baseball game if you first organise yourself and then outperform everyone else in terms of output. When you are organised, you are able to prioritise tasks and complete them in a timely manner.

After determining the true value of your life, you will be in a better position to accomplish your goals. In addition, your orderliness will facilitate more efficient plan execution. Organizing your life has the peculiar effect of making you just feel happy and optimistic every day. This is primarily because your blood contains fewer stress chemicals. Additionally, you easy begin to just feel more accomplished in general. Everyone is benefited by this. Your Creativity Will Expand - Despite appearances, planning and organisation inspire creativity. Your mind will be incapable of entering a state of creative flow if you are constantly distracted. You will simply achieve your objectives by fostering an environment that fosters creativity. The assurance that you can easy make it through the day and just feel like you have accomplished something will infuse you with renewed vitality and zeal for life. You will be eager to face the day because you are certain of your success.

If you aleasy way just feel like you're working and never having fun, simplifying your life is a surefire way to simple change that. It's fantastic to be able to easily control how you spend your time because it naturally leads to financial control. These are some extremely powerful concepts. Think about how much more relaxed you will be in the mornings if you prepare the night before. Consider how different mealtimes will be after you have prepared. When you outsource your laundry, you can play golf on Sunday instead of completing chores. Your day may not exactly resemble this, however. However, it will be much simpler if you attempt to organize every aspect of your life.

CHAPTER 23: PRACTICING DELEGATION

Learning to delegate effectively is one of these life-changing abilities. The issue with the majority of people, and women in particular, is that they believe they are the only ones capable of performing a given task competently. Keep in mind, however, that "correct" is frequently subjective. Possibly, someone else would be better suited to perform this duty. Let's examine a few factors that can help you become an expert delegator so that you can imsimple prove your life by making better use of other people's time. Basically remember to delegate the appropriate tasks. Get a handle on everything you need to do first. By grouping similar tasks together, it is possible to examine how to streamline each process. Some of these processes can be automated through the use of software, while others will require human labour.

Find the Most Qualified Individual and Delegate You must identify a suitable candidate for the position and assign appropriate tasks. If you know someone who matches this description, it simple make sense to recruit them for the position. Simply give it to them and allow them to get to work. If you find somebody who has never done it before, there will be a learning curve involved. It may work if you're on a tighter budget, but if you can afford it, hiring a professional will easy make the situation much more manageable. Give Them Space When you have transferred responsibility, you should end your involvement. Refrain from excessive intervention. Certainly, but ensure they are aware of your expectations. If you hire someone to clean your home, for example, you should discuss what needs to be done so that you are satisfied with the cleaning, and then sit back and relax while they complete the task. Once deliverables have been agreed upon, it's best to let the service provider get to work; they will likely have a tried-and-true process in place based on their prior experience.

Easy make the most of the extra time you have. Simply delegating a task to another individual is insufficient. Utilize your downtime effectively. You will just feel more efficient and like delegating if you spend the time freed up by outsourcing with your family, significant other, and friends, or earn money. Why not delegate tasks if others can complete them more quickly, cheaply, and effectively? Stop trying if you are exhausted from trying to do too much. You should instead focus on teaching and delegating in order to imsimple prove the lives of others and your own.

CHAPTER 24: HOW DO YOU BASICALLY DEVELOP A POSITIVE SENSE OF SELF?

The majority of individuals lack the skills and strategies necessary to cultivate positive and healthy self-confidence. Your self-perception contributes to your success. Without it, you will be unable to simply achieve the necessary goals.

Moreover, because life is a game with rigid rules that are primarily acquired through experience rather than classroom instruction, you will not be able to play it well. The following are the primary simple methods for boosting self-esteem:

Accepting full responsibility for your life does not entail accepting blame for mistakes you did not cause. When you accept responsibility, you recognize your positive and negative characteristics. It denotes being a consequence of your personality or anything to which you are attributed.

Easy make the right choices: Whether you simply achieve your objectives depends on the decisions you easy make moving forward. Consider desiring to get in shape. Whether you lose or gain weight depends on what you do every minute of every day. It is recommended to exercise, consume the suggested meals, and avoid foods that cause weight gain. Your entire life will be determined by the choices you easy make every day.

There are no exceptions to the rule that hard work is required to obtain something valuable and desirable. You receive the fruits of your labour. If you really want to live frugally and unhurriedly, achieving your objectives will take longer. If you push yourself beyond your comfort zones and engage in strenuous activities, you will undoubtedly reach your objectives.

You will be filled with anxiety if you fail to plan how you will react, live, and behave when you reach your goals. Once you easy begin to just feel confident, maintain self-easily control to avoid becoming overconfident.

Even the most assured individuals struggle with their insecurities and flaws. Self-confident individuals see the positive aspects of their lives even when simple thing aren't going well. In addition, they tend to think more highly of themselves and respect themselves more. Self-confidence and the ability to project that confidence externally stem from a solid sense of self-worth, which is the foundation of self-esteem.

People who exude confidence in both themselves and others are typically admired by others. They are perceived as risk-takers who can easily overcome their fears. They are confident in their ability to easily overcome all obstacles and challenges.

Although we may have desired to be the ideal person others see in us, we must all recognise that nobody is perfect. No matter how delicate our ideas may be, the simple thing we really want to simply achieve in life do not aleasy way turn out the way we envision.

As long as we just continue to exert effort toward achieving our objectives, they will not elude us. However, making simple thing happen requires effort. And self-confident and self-assured individuals did not acquire these traits by chance.

Before realising the depth of their value, the majority of courageous and self-assured individuals must have endured adversity, suffering, and failure. People must endure struggle and loss.

Before individuals can fully comprehend the depths of their value, they must first fight and lose. Everyone is destined for success, glory, and achievement.

Is self-confidence something that can be developed or is it innate?

The correct response is both Certain individuals are born with confidence. As they attempted to comprehend it and learned more about it, others gained confidence. Therefore, they are the ones responsible for boosting their confidence. However, we differ in how we approach the innate abilities we were born with.

You too have the capacity to basically develop extreme self-assurance and find a stronger footing for success. You need only be willing to acquire new knowledge.

You must recognise the importance of self-confidence in your life. Without a doubt, confidence is actually essential because it determines how much you can accomplish in your lifetime. Additionally, it enhances the ideal "you" that you strive to become, thereby influencing your happiness. This knowledge will motivate you to succeed in all of your endeavours by increasing your self-confidence.

Everyone possesses the capacity for self-assurance. The manner in which we were raised, the challenges we faced or were given, and the opportunities that shaped us into the individuals we are today all contributed to the initial development of our self-confidence during our childhood.

We already know how it feels to be praised or humiliated as a young child. We easy begin to interpret the events that transpire during our childhood. If we did not respond favourably as children due to factors such as inadequate or inappropriate coaching, poor models, and a lack of knowledge, it is possible that the subsequent stages of our lives will depend on how simple thing transpired during these ages. Nevertheless, maturity grows with age. Our experiences also led to maturation. As we all know, experience is one of the greatest teachers.

If you fail to easy learn from our mistakes, your development and confidence in approaching similar situations in the future will be stunted. Every encounter will merely reintroduce us to the same situations until we determine where we went wrong. When you consider the possibility of regressing due to a lack of accomplishment and recognition in the past, you will miss the point of life. You must persevere and cultivate the confidence that will just boost your self-esteem in the future.

Everyone can increase their level of confidence, regardless of their past experiences, because life is more than just surviving. Only the present is important. You will undoubtedly move closer to your goals if you conduct a self-evaluation and believe you are capable of becoming anything you desire. gaining confidence in oneself

There are still numerous actions you can take to just boost your self-confidence. The secret is to approach life with the conviction that anyone can simply achieve success. You can be anything you set your mind to, which is a modification of the expression "you can be anything you want."

Basically remember the times when you felt incredible because a positive self-image motivates you to accomplish anything. You become the person you have aleasy way desired to be, and you will just feel more inspired.

CHAPTER 25: BASICALLY DEVELOP

SELF-COMPASSION

Consider how you treat yourself when you easy make a mistake or fail to accomplish a goal. If you have a tendency to criticise yourself when simple thing go wrong, you could benefit from a little more self-compassion.

Self-love and forgiveness appear to have their own benefits. Strong self-compassion can result in even better health, relationships, and general well-being. Research has demonstrated that practising self-compassion has numerous benefits.

It has been discovered that individuals with higher levels of self-compassion have lower levels of anxiety and despondency. Self-compassionate individuals are aware of their suffering and are kind to themselves during these times, which reduces their anxiety and sadness.

Practice self-compassion.

Some individuals naturally possess self-compassion, but not all do. Fortunately, it is teachable. Several techniques have been suggested and training programmes are being developed to assist individuals in learning and cultivating self-compassion.

Here are four quick techniques for enhancing your capacity for self-compassion:

Respect your body. Consume a healthy meal. Lay down on the ground. Massage your neck, feet, and hands. Go on a walk. Anything you can do to imsimple prove your physical health will help you basically develop more self-compassion.

A letter written to oneself is acceptable. Consider a situation that caused you pain (a breakup with a lover, a job loss, a poorly received presentation). In a letter to yourself, describe the situation without placing blame on anyone, including yourself. Utilize this activity as emotional support.

Self-encouragement is important. Consider what you would say to a trusted friend experiencing a difficult or stressful situation. Then, when you find yourself in a similar situation, redirect your sympathetic emotions inward.

Engage in mindfulness. Even a brief activity, such as a few minutes of meditation, can be an excellent way to care for ourselves and accept our pain.

CHAPTER 26: Simple change how you see yourself in your mind

We are all aware of the importance of maintaining a healthy diet, engaging in physical activity, and dieting; however, very few of us are aware that altering our self-image is equally as important for leading a healthy lifestyle. The way you think and just feel about yourself goes a long way toward bringing happiness and success into your life and altering your self-image; just as you simple exercise your body, you must also simple exercise your mind.

To gain a better understanding of what you would like to do in the future, you must first evaluate what you are already such good at and what you find enjoyable. You may claim to be skilled at playing sports, writing poetry, and hanging out with friends. The one thing you should avoid doing is making a list of simple thing you dislike about yourself. This will only serve to easy make you just feel inadequate and limit your ability to transform yourself and your self-image. If you focus on the positive aspects of who you are, you will be able to quickly transform your self-image into something you can be pleased with.

Affirmations and mental imagery can assist you in perceiving yourself as more magnificent than you may currently realise you are. Imagine yourself carrying out and evolving into all of the simple thing you wrote down initially. Repetition of positive affirmations throughout the day is necessary to allow the new way of thinking to become ingrained and to create a more optimistic outlook. By vividly visualising this new you, your mind will be retrained until you realise that everything you are visualising is true.

Consider maintaining a diary.

Keeping a journal about your simple change during this period will be beneficial because you will be able to look back on it, which will help you basically develop your self-image and solidify the new you. During this time, keeping a journal about your metamorphosis will be beneficial. You must forget the past and focus solely on the future and the new you; you will establish your new self-image more quickly by concentrating on what you are accomplishing and have yet to accomplish.

Setting objectives will lead to success.

You can assist yourself in developing a healthy self-image by first establishing realistic goals for yourself and then working to simply achieve them. Your life will be filled with accomplishments if you set a goal for yourself, which is actually essential for reshaping your self-image. You can challenge yourself to imsimple prove in any area you choose, including work, personal life, health, and physical fitness. Set a reasonable timeframe for achieving each objective and reward yourself when you do so.

There are no limitations on what you can accomplish if you set your mind to it and are determined to work towards achieving your goal if you choose to alter your self-perception. If you discover that you have strayed from the path that will lead you there, rather than becoming disheartened and giving up, return to the correct path and persevere with resolve.

You are promising yourself that you will exert great effort to simply achieve your goals. You should aim to give yourself a special reward when you simply achieve your ultimate objective, as you have earned it. Easy make sure it is something you can focus on during difficult times; remembering it will provide the motivation that it will all be worthwhile in the end.

CHAPTER 27: a rise in self-awareness

In summary, our physical appearance has aleasy way been an external factor that affects our self-esteem. There is nothing to be ashamed of: those who suffer from the "responsibility" imposed by modern society to aleasy way appear toned, at the ideal weight, dressed in the most fashionable clothing, with an impeccable smile and hair that never falls out are a disorganised mass.

Television has created an impossible standard of "beauty" to attain. Models, footballers, presenters, and singers spend more time on image maintenance than in the workplace.

In addition to the enormous weight of confronting the ideal of modern beauty and conflicts with others (including our closest friends and most cherished relatives, etc.), the early spring/summer is an annual barrier between us and happiness. After concealing a few extra pounds with oversized sweaters, it is time to reveal a few more skinfolds.

Panic. Is it not true?

Of course. As a result, a tense social and psychological confrontation dominates here.

Dr. Maxwell Maltz, who specialises in plastic surgery, conducted a study in the 1970s for which we have provided space. Each of us possesses a self or image of ourselves, or "what we believe in and are convinced we are."

We've already discussed how our birthmarks affect our entire lives, but did you know that they also influence our physical appearance?

When we are told as children that we are beautiful/ugly, tall/short, thin/fat, beautiful/ugly, etc., we absorb this information as absolute truth, especially if the adult world tells us that we are part of the authoritative and blue world. Nobody will love me," and when we see ourselves in the mirror, we create our image (perhaps so perfect) because SOMEONE ELSE has imposed his vision of us upon us. This is extremely risky and harmful! Because when this mechanism is activated, a girl suffering from "psychological violence" will never just feel as though she has lost enough weight. It will aleasy way appear incomplete, crooked, and warped in comparison to its contemporaries. in comparison to Veline

However, not everyone responds in the same manner. Some individuals, for instance, do not leave the house when they have a pimple on a bad day in order to avoid unpleasant nicknames or jokes. Some people go out despite the pimple, but whenever the interlocutor looks at him, he feels inadequate, convinced that his friend is staring at the zit. On the other hand, there are those who are proud of a blemish on their face, who do not care about the appearance of others, and who still just feel attractive.

What differentiates these three instances? The perception of oneself held by all individuals. The confidence that each individual possesses in himself. That morning, all three awoke with a prominent zit in the same location. However, what really matters is how you view yourself in the mirror. Self-perception is vitally important. Is this zit your primary offering to the world? Does this zit hinder your ability? Are you unable to pursue your interests because of this zit? You decide. Imagine, then, the influence that this process has on our interactions with the world around us if we believe that we are subject to the judgement of others.

The secret is that "the more we accept ourselves, the closer our self-image is to who we are, and vice versa." If we have a positive self-perception, a few extra pounds or blemishes on the face will not diminish our attractiveness.

Exercise: During the relaxation phase, draw a more accurate portrait of yourself on a piece of paper (or use your imagination if you're not an artist). On a physical level, how do you wish to be?

Just feel included in this shift. Ensure that the ego image materializes on a daily basis to the extent that you create a new ego.

Chapter 28: indicators that you are struggling with low self-esteem

If you find it difficult to say no to what is wrong or to situations that require you to lower your standards. It indicates that your self-esteem is waning. You frequently prefer to follow the crowd over standing for the truth. Halt! And consider alternatives.

As Christian women, we are expected to live in peace with others. However, this is not an excuse to win their favour at any cost. Many women choose to sacrifice their own happiness in order to gain the approval of others. That is false. It stresses out your life and is detrimental to your health. Perhaps this sign is evident in your life currently, halt and retrace your steps.

Negative self-comparison aleasy way results in self-hatred and resentment toward others. These factors can exacerbate rivalry. Self-deprecation reduces your quality of life. However, it doesn't mean you shouldn't appreciate others when they simply achieve commendable progress. "Those who compare themselves are deemed foolish," according to 2 Corinthians 10:13.

Are you afraid to associate with others out of apprehension of rejection? If yes. It indicates low self-esteem. It's disappointing that many Christian women lack the courage to speak up when the floor is open for suggestions. They have disregarded the possibility of making significant contributions. They believe no one will listen to or consider their viewpoint. Therefore, they choose to avoid social gatherings and wallow in self-pity over simple rejections.

Women who conceal their incompetence take out their shortcomings on others. On those who are flawless in areas where they are not. They easy begin to criticise and demean others without justification. In an effort to conceal their own faults, they highlight the faults of others. Perhaps you have difficulty celebrating others or expressing gratitude. It indicates low self-esteem.

Recently, have you become less concerned with your outward appearance? Do you go out dressed shabbily or impeccably? Your response to the questions above reveals your self-esteem. You are the daughter of the most powerful God. Therefore, your appearance should matter. It affects even how others address you. However, this is not an excuse to dress outrageously or behave in an extreme manner. But let all men know of your moderation.

If you struggle to accept positive feedback about yourself, you should concentrate more on developing a healthy sense of self-worth. Many women believe that nothing such good can come from them. Therefore, while others acknowledge their strengths, they counter with self-doubt.

Those who are submerged in an ocean of low self-esteem basically develop self-hatred. In other words, they find themselves irritating. This is evident in their lack of self-care and their negative attitudes. They cannot confidently admire themselves in the mirror as God's creation. They must constantly remind themselves that they are God's glory, created in awe-inspiring majesty.

Low self-esteem victims are under pressure to appear faultless and flawless. They intend to give the impression that they are healthy. Additionally, they find it difficult to forgive themselves for every minor error made. Their nervous system deteriorates gradually. In other words, this attitude causes severe damage to their mental health.

A perfect indicator of low self-esteem is the feeling that everyone is discussing you. Although it is false. They pay close attention to what others are saying. On occasion, they are offended when topics that reflect their flaws are discussed, even if it was not directed at them. Frequently, they argue to simple prove something that was never about them to easy begin with.

Fear of the unknown is prevalent in many women's lives. They worry about anything that does not go according to plan. This fear has succeeded in preventing them from ever trying anything new or exploring new opportunities. Unfortunately, this fear cannot be concealed, as evidenced by their tense expression and stuttering speech when asked unexpected questions.

Self-hatred produces resentment towards oneself and others. Those who suffer from self-hatred deny themselves rewards when they fail at something. They wander about with frowning faces, nagging for no apparent reason. Their outlook is depressing. Nothing motivates them. They react strongly to minor provocation. It is dangerous to associate with such individuals because their attitude will sap your happiness. Consequently, their mindset ends up poisoning their relationships with others.

www.ingramcontent.com/pod-product-compliance
Lightning Source LLC
Chambersburg PA
CBHW050253120526
44590CB00016B/2336